Diana su l'Elba

Recent Researches in Music

A-R Editions publishes seven series of critical editions, spanning the history of Western music, American music, and oral traditions.

Recent Researches in the Music of the Middle Ages and Early Renaissance
    Charles M. Atkinson, general editor

Recent Researches in the Music of the Renaissance
    James Haar, general editor

Recent Researches in the Music of the Baroque Era
    Christoph Wolff, general editor

Recent Researches in the Music of the Classical Era
    Eugene K. Wolf, general editor

Recent Researches in the Music of the Nineteenth and Early Twentieth Centuries
    Rufus Hallmark, general editor

Recent Researches in American Music
    John M. Graziano, general editor

Recent Researches in the Oral Traditions of Music
    Philip V. Bohlman, general editor

Each edition in *Recent Researches* is devoted to works by a single composer or to a single genre. The content is chosen for its high quality and historical importance, and each edition includes a substantial introduction and critical report. The music is engraved according to the highest standards of production using the proprietary software MusE, owned by MusicNotes, Inc.

For information on establishing a standing order to any of our series, or for editorial guidelines on submitting proposals, please contact:

A-R Editions, Inc.
801 Deming Way
Madison, Wisconsin 53717

800 736-0070 (U.S. book orders)
608 836-9000 (phone)
608 831-8200 (fax)
http://www.areditions.com

Johann David Heinichen

JUN 1 9 2000

Diana su l'Elba

Edited by Michael Walter

 A-R Editions, Inc.

Madison

A-R Editions, Inc., Madison, Wisconsin 53717
© 2000 by A-R Editions, Inc.

A-R Editions is pleased to support scholars and performers
in their use of *Recent Researches* material for study or performance. Subscribers to any of the *Recent Researches* series,
as well as patrons of subscribing institutions, are invited to
apply for information about our "Copyright Sharing
Policy."

Printed in the United States of America

ISBN 0-89579-453-5
ISSN 0484-0828

Contents

Acknowledgments

I owe thanks to Michael Werner for his help in preparing the introduction and David Spencer for his help in preparing the English translation of the libretto. Dr. Karl Wilhelm Geck, head of the Department of Music of the Sächsische Landesbibliothek—Staats- und Universitäts-bibliothek Dresden, gave the permission to publish the edition. He and his staff were very helpful and pleasant during my work there. Prof. Dr. Wolfram Steude gave helpful advice. The initial archival research was made possible by a travel grant of the Fritz Thyssen Stiftung. Petra Kloh was an indefatigable help in the sometimes difficult task of copying materials. Last but not least, I wish to thank Dr. Claudia Schnitzer who instigated and supported my research, of which this edition is a part.

Introduction

The Dresden Wedding Festivities of 1719

In August 1719 the Saxon prince Friedrich August (II) was married in Vienna to Maria Josepha, archduchess and daughter of Joseph I. There were, as usual, political reasons for the marriage. By this union, the Saxon elector Friedrich August I (King August II in Poland, "the Strong") tied the house of Saxony to the house of Habsburg and sought to raise his rank among the European kings.

August the Strong had planned the marriage since 1711. In that year there was a chance that the archduchess, born in 1699, would become heir of the Habsburg lands ("Erblande"). Her father, Joseph I, had died in 1711, and according to the rules of succession (*Pactum mutuae successionis*), his brother Karl VI followed him as heir and was elected emperor. According to the same rules, it was possible that Maria Josepha, the eldest daughter of Joseph I, would inherit the Habsburg lands if Karl VI died without leaving a son. (The *Pactum* was ambiguous, as it was not clear whether Maria Josepha or an eldest daughter who might be born to Karl VI would be heir.) Under these circumstances, a marriage between Friedrich August (II) and Maria Josepha could mean that the son of August the Strong would become de facto heir of the Habsburg lands and possibly emperor. Since Karl VI was no fool, he tried to secure the succession for his own children by means of the *Pragmatische Sanktion* (1713), which interpreted the *Pactum* in a way that his own daughter would become his heir. Karl had no children until 1716, when his wife gave birth to a son, who later died in 1717. In the same year, however, Karl's daughter, Maria Theresia, was born and superseded Maria Josepha in the line of succession. It was only then that August the Strong's son was welcomed in Vienna as future bridegroom of Maria Josepha. In the marriage contract, August the Strong renounced any hereditary title concerning the Habsburg territory.[1]

August the Strong himself planned the wedding celebrations of 1719, studying older festival books as guides. He sought to sum up the Habsburg and the Saxon traditions of festivities so that the celebrations would reflect the joining of the two houses and the creation of a new dynasty, which he hoped would rival that of Austria and France.[2] Under the reign of August the Strong before 1717, the predominant cultural forms in Dresden were French. It might be, as it is sometimes stated in the secondary literature, that August the Strong, who had visited Paris in his youth, was fond of French music and French tragedy. We cannot be sure, however, for we can refer only to the cultural image that August wished to project to other European courts. Since he tried to establish absolutist power according to the model of the French King Louis XIV, August preferred a French cultural image for political reasons. Once the marriage plan was finalized, it seemed necessary to change this cultural image in order to demonstrate the new rank of the house of Saxony as relatives of the Austrian emperor. Because in Vienna the predominant cultural guises were Italian, August looked for a chance to establish Italian opera in Dresden. Perhaps the prince-elector, in his journeys to Italy, developed "a taste for the arts of that country."[3] But surely, that caprice alone would not have caused August the Strong, encumbered with debts and confronted with the need to finance the venture by raising an additional loan of nearly 30,000 taler, to engage in 1717 a very expensive Italian opera company, which not only included singers and instrumentalists but also the composer Antonio Lotti, the poet Antonio Maria Luchini, the architect Alessandro Mauro, plus two painters and two carpenters. (Johann David Heinichen had already been engaged as court kapellmeister in 1716.) The predominantly Italian character of the wedding celebrations demonstrated August the Strong's newly gained political rank as elector of Saxony and king in Poland, rather than representing his personal tastes. (French culture was not rejected entirely, however; the celebrations included French ballets between opera acts, a French opera-ballet, and French tragedies.)

Therefore the engagement of Lotti, a composer renowned for the publication of a volume of *Duetti, terzetti, e madrigali a più voci*[4] dedicated to the Austrian Emperor Joseph I, was not a coincidence. Lotti was also one of the most celebrated opera composers of his time. Among the singers engaged were Santa Scarabelli Stella, Lotti's wife and a famous soprano, the castratos Senesino (Francesco Bernardi) and Matteo Berselli, and the bass Giuseppe Maria Boschi. Additionally, in 1718 violinist Francesco Maria Veracini, theorbo virtuoso Silvius Leopold Weiss, and, among others, the singers Margherita Durastanti, Antonia Maria Novelli Laurenti ("La Coralli"), and Vittoria Tesi were engaged.[5] At the time the Italian company was engaged, the Hofkapelle already was one of the outstanding orchestras in Europe.

According to Johann Joachim Quantz who visited Dresden in March 1716,

> The Royal Orchestra at that time was already in a particularly flourishing state. Through the French equal style of execution introduced by [Jean Baptiste] Volumier, the concertmaster at that time,[6] it already distinguished itself from many other orchestras; and later, under the direction of the following concertmaster, Mr. [Johann Georg] Pisendel, it achieved, through the introduction of a mixed style, such refinement of performance that, in all my later travels, I heard none better.[7]

To perform Lotti's Italian *opere serie*, August the Strong decided to build a new opera house, the famous opera house at the "Zwinger" (a complex of buildings intended for festival purposes surrounding a wide courtyard), of which Matthäus Daniel Pöppelmann was the architect and for which Mauro created the vast stage and interior decorations.[8] Construction began in summer 1718; Count Wackerbarth announced the completion of the opera house to August the Strong on 25 August 1719; and it was inaugurated with a performance of Lotti's *Giove in Argo*, which was part of the wedding celebrations, on 3 September.[9] The opera house was one of the largest in Europe and could accommodate an audience of up to two thousand people. Seventy-six men alone were needed as stagehands.

After the marriage in Vienna, Maria Josepha entered the territory of Saxony on 2 September 1719; nearly the entire month was subsequently filled with wedding festivities (see table 1). Nobles came to Dresden from Saxony and all over Europe to attend the celebrations. Many musicians also came, including Pier Francesco Tosi, George Frideric Handel, and Georg Philipp Telemann.[10] Until the nineteenth century the famous festivities and ceremonies served as models for other European courts.[11] To understand the context in which *Diana su l'Elba* (Diana on the Elbe)[12] and *La Gara degli Dei* (The Competition of the Gods)[13] were performed, as well as their purpose, it is necessary to give a short account of the festivities.

On Saturday, 2 September, the bride approached from Pirna, a small town at the Elbe, on an imitation of the Venetian vessel *Buccentauro*.[14] Some famous musicians from the Hofkapelle (Pantaleon Hebenstreit, Pierre-Gabriel Buffardin, and Silvius Leopold Weiss) together with six oboists and two hornists rode on the vessel in order to welcome the archduchess with music. The next day there was a solemn Te Deum in the Catholic chapel of the court[15] with the participation of members of the court trumpet corps (as was usual on solemn occasions) and a gala dinner in the palace, accompanied by instrumental and vocal music. That evening Lotti's opera, *Giove in Argo*, was performed. On Monday, 4 September, there was a ball in the "Riesensaal" (giants' hall, which referred to larger-than-life figures of warriors painted on the walls) of the palace, lasting from 7 P.M. to 4 A.M. the following morning. A French tragedy was performed on the evening of the same day. On Wednesday, 6 September, there was a "Kampf-Jagen" (wild beast fight), a special form of the hunt that took place in a big, wooden amphitheater (the audience numbered more than four thousand people). Several wild animals were sent into the amphitheater, among them a lion and a lioness, a panther, a baboon, six bears, wild boars, and aurochs. The beasts were to mangle one another before some of them were shot by the elector (the wife of August the Strong did not attend the "Kampf-Jagen"), his son, and the archduchess. (Unfortunately, the expectations of the spectators were not fulfilled because most of the animals did not hurt each other. The king and the archduchess shot some wild sows while the prince-elector shot a bear.) The "Kampf-Jagen" was announced by trumpeters and timpanists; then hunting music, which has not survived, was played. On the evening of the same day an Italian comedy was performed, and on the evening of the next day Lotti's opera, *Ascanio* (1718). On Friday and Saturday, 8 and 9 September, a "Maintenator-Rennen" (running at a ring, in which mounted nobles with lances charged at rings attached to a pillar) took place in the courtyard of the stables, preceded by a procession of nobles and participants in the manner of many other festivities. It was followed on each evening by an Italian and a French comedy, respectively. On Wednesday, 13 September, the first performance of Lotti's famous opera, *Teofane*, took place (and was repeated on Thursday, 21 September, and Wednesday, 27 September); it was composed specially for the wedding and had been in rehearsal since June.[16] Sunday, 17 September, was devoted to the Turkish feast, for which a band played janissary music. The Hofkapelle also provided music for the gala dinner, possibly including a concerto by Telemann.[17] The feast was followed that night by a "Nacht-Schießen" (nocturnal shooting match) in which nobles shot at targets on a lavishly illuminated field. Once a target was hit, a small firework was set off.

The festivities of the seven planets comprised the core of the wedding celebrations, with each of the planetary gods serving as patron for a different festivity.[18] The first festivity was that of the Sun on Sunday, 10 September, introduced by Heinichen's *La Gara degli Dei* and concluded by a fireworks display based on a plot described at the end of the libretto. As we know from two drawings, the singers portraying the gods sat in a machine (or possibly a decoration), which represented a cloud above the orchestra, in the garden of the so-called Dutch Palace on the bank of the river Elbe.[19] In one of the drawings a theorbo player, presumably the famous Silvius Leopold Weiss who played the theorbo part in Saturno's aria "I rapidi Vanni," stands in front of the orchestra. Mars was the patron of the second planetary festivity on Tuesday, 12 September, when a mounted and foot tournament took place.[20] August the Strong himself appeared as Mars, dressed in Roman armor. On Friday, 15 September, Jupiter presided over the Carousel of the Four Elements, which inaugurated the Zwinger and was "meant as a delicate compliment to the Habsburg bride," for it referred to the *Contesa dell'arie e dell'acqua* held in Vienna in 1667.[21] Although the Carousel resembled the Italian tournament-opera, it was essentially a running at the head and the ring:

Date (Day of Week)	Feast and Activities	Major Musical Events
2 (Saturday)	Maria Josepha travels by ship (*Buccentauro*) from Pirna to Dresden	musicians on the ship: Pierre-Gabriel Buffardin, Silvius Leopold Weiss, and Pantaleon Hebenstreit, as well as oboists and hornists
3 (Sunday)	at noon, solemn Te Deum in the Catholic Court Chapel; 330 shots fired off from cannons during the Te Deum	court trumpet corps
	gala dinner ("Solemne Tafel") in the palace	Hofkapelle and singers ("Capelmusique und Operisten")
	in the evening an *opera pastorale*	performance of Lotti's *Giove in Argo*
4 (Monday)	ball	dance music, with 94 musicians
5 (Tuesday)	French play, *Ariane*	
6 (Wednesday)	"Kampf-Jagen" (wild beast fight)	
	in the evening an Italian play	
7 (Thursday)	opera	performance of Lotti's *Ascanio*
8 (Friday)	"Maintenator-Rennen" (charging at the ring)	
	in the evening an Italian play	
9 (Saturday)	continuation of the "Maintenator-Rennen"	
	in the evening a French play, *l'Inconnue*	
10 (Sunday)	**Feast of the Sun** fireworks display	performance of Heinichen's *La Gara degli Dei*; beginning of the fireworks display is announced by 64 trumpeters and 8 timpanists
	later in the evening table music	table music
11 (Monday)	French play, *Hypermnestre*	
12 (Tuesday)	**Feast of Mars** mounted and foot tournament	
	in the evening a play	
13 (Wednesday)	"Große Italiänische Opera"	performance of Lotti's *Teofane*
14 (Thursday)	in the evening a French play	
15 (Friday)	**Feast of Jupiter** Carousel of the Four Elements; horse ballet	before the Carousel of the Four Elements: performance of Lotti's cantata, *Li quattro Elementi* accompaniment of the horse ballet by military musicians (among them 32 oboists and 6 hornists)
	in the evening an Italian play	

Date (Day of Week)	Feast and Activities	Major Musical Events
16 (Saturday)	day of rest (August the Strong participated in a hunt at Pillnitz)	
	in the evening dancing in the theater	dance music
17 (Sunday)	Turkish feast	table music and janissary music
	"Nacht-Schießen" (nocturnal shooting match)	
18 (Monday)	**Feast of Diana** aquatic hunt	performance of Heinichen's *Diana su l'Elba*
	in the evening an Italian play	
19 (Tuesday)	day of rest	(Lotti's *Teofane* was scheduled to be performed but had to be cancelled because one of the singers felt ill)
20 (Wednesday)	**Feast of Mercury** Fair of the Nations	procession with the Hofkapelle (and additional musicians, presumably)
21 (Thursday)	"Große Opera"	performance of Lotti's *Teofane*
22 (Friday)	Italian (or French) play	
23 (Saturday)	**Feast of Venus** the ladies' running at the ring; subsequently gala dinner; ball in the temple of Venus	dance music
	"Ballet von Dames u. Cavalliers"	performance of Schmidt's *Les quatre saisons*
24 (Sunday)	opera	performance of Lotti's *Ascanio*
25 (Monday)	French (or Italian) play	
26 (Tuesday)	**Feast of Saturn** Miners' festivity	a singer represents Saturn (presumably in a minor cantata by Lotti); table music follows in two adjoining rooms
	"Klopf-Jagen" (dragnet hunt)	
27 (Wednesday)	"Neue Italiänische Opera"	performance of Lotti's *Teofane*
28 (Thursday)	Italian play	
29 (Friday)	opera	performance of Lotti's *Ascanio*

*The timetable was compiled on the basis of the court's official timetable. Additionally, the following were consulted: the *Hof-Journal* of September 1719; the timetable in Gress, 135–49; and the royal monument of the festivities, the title page of which reads: "Das Königliche | Denckmal, | Welches Nach geschehener Vermäh-lung | Ihro Hoheit des Königlichen und | Chur=Sächsischen | Kron=Printzens | Herrn Friedrich Augusti, | Mit der Durchlauchtigsten | Fr. Maria Josepha, | Ertz=Hertzogin von Oesterreich, | Bey Dero | Hohen Ankunfft | In der Königl. und Chur=Sächs. | Residentz=Stadt | Dreßden, | Vom ersten bis letzten Sept. 1719. gestiftet | wor-den" (Frankfurt/Leipzig, 1719). There are some minor differences in the sources, so I have chosen the most probable version without further discussion.

The Carousel begins with the entry of Jupiter seated on a machine, designed by Alessandro Mauro, who was responsible for the costumes generally in 1719. The machine, which represented Chaos, could emit fire, earth, air and water all together. Jupiter . . . sings an aria, the machine moves aside and the combatants can enter.[22]

(The singer who represented Jupiter in the cantata, *Li quattro elementi*, for which the music is lost, was the bass Giuseppe Maria Boschi, who also sang the role of Emireno in Lotti's *Teofane*.)

Monday, 18 September, was the day of Diana and featured a "Wasser-Jagen" (aquatic hunt): four hundred animals, mostly deer and some wild boars and sows, were forced into the river Elbe near the palace to be shot by the hunters. At 2 P.M., before the hunt, a gilded and silvered ship approached, "drawn" by four "Wasser-Pferde" (water horses, presumably floating statues attached to the ship) and carrying the musicians and singers who performed Heinichen's *Diana su l'Elba*.[23] All of the singers wore green costumes.[24] Hunting festivities played an important role in celebrations because of the prince-elector and the archduchess's famous fondness for the hunt. Mercury's festivity on Wednesday, 20 September, was introduced with a procession and possibly another Italian cantata;[25] it continued with a great Fair of the Nations and a lottery in the Zwinger.[26] On Saturday, 23 September, the festivity of Venus took place, for which the main event was the ladies' charging at the ring. Afterward the court attended the French opera-ballet, *Les quatre saisons*, composed by Johann Christoph Schmidt (the court's senior kapellmeister) and performed by nobles in the outdoor theater in the Großer Garten. In the evening the nobles attended a ball in the temple of Venus, a newly erected (presumably wooden) building with large "windows" to give people in the amphitheater-like building housing the temple the opportunity to see the noble ball. The last festivity honored Saturn on Tuesday, 26 September. Known as the "Miners' festivity," it included a procession, a hunt, singing by the miners, an Italian comedy, and a ball. A singer and a small orchestra performed in the dome of the hall representing Saturn's temple; other orchestras played in two adjoining rooms. The wedding celebrations were concluded with a performance of Lotti's *Ascanio* on Friday, 29 September. Virtually all of the festivities had music, ranging from fanfares played by trumpets and timpani (which were also part of the processions), performances of military bands (consisting mainly of oboes), and dance and table music (played by the Hofkapelle) to major vocal works like *La Gara degli Dei* and *Teofane*.

The Composer

Johann David Heinichen (1683–1729), son of a pastor, was a pupil of and later assistant to Johann Kuhnau at the Leipzig Thomasschule before he enrolled in 1702 at Leipzig University where he studied law.[27] Working in Weissenfels as advocate after finishing his studies, Heinichen occasionally composed music for the court. Returning to Leipzig in 1709, he composed several operas for the Leipzig Opera House and was appointed composer at the court of Zeitz and opera composer at the court of Naumburg. In 1710 Heinichen left Leipzig for Venice in order to become familiar with the modern Venetian style. During his sojourn he was commissioned to write two operas (*Mario* and *Le passioni per troppo amore*) that were said to have been performed successfully, but since we know of no other Italian operas written by Heinichen in Italy, there remain reasonable doubts concerning the success of both works. In Venice he came into contact with leading composers, including Lotti, Carlo Francesco Pollaroli, Francesco Gasparini, and Antonio Vivaldi; he also met Gottfried Heinrich Stölzel, who travelled through Italy. Most of Heinichen's activities in Italy remain unknown. We know only that in 1712 he travelled to Rome, where he gave music lessons to Prince Leopold of Anhalt-Cöthen, who later would become Johann Sebastian Bach's patron. In Venice Heinichen composed at least one concerto, several cantatas, a serenade, and the oratorio *La pace di Kamberga*, which was dedicated to the prince-elector of Saxony and presumably supported an application to be composer for the Dresden Hofkapelle.

Heinichen was appointed electoral kapellmeister in August 1716 (a post he retained until his death) but stayed in Venice with the prince-elector until the end of that year. Heinichen's modern style was attractive to the Dresden court, for the fame of any Hofkapelle depended upon a fashionable repertory. (This might have contributed to the lack of interest in J. S. Bach's music in Dresden.) In 1717 Heinichen wrote a letter to Johann Mattheson in Hamburg that showed he considered himself part of the avant garde of his time:

> I willingly admit that I often have pondered why there are still people in our time who try to maintain and defend the long-expired rules of past times. In my opinion, the most important reasons are [the following]: first, those musical Mr. Antiquarians have spent most of their early years or their entire lives with such whims, and they by no means want [to believe] that they have learned them in vain. Yes, since too much time would be lost in [their] thinking further about the subject, they find it agreeable to be like those pious mothers who love only the children [who were] most difficult to deliver. Second, for those holding onto these prejudices, it seems all Greek if one says to them that, today, subtle and clever rules and lengthy praxis are more necessary for touching ear music than [they are] for heart-attacking eye music, which, on the innocent sheet of paper, is tortured according to the rules of the venerable counterpoints of the Mr. Cantors of the smallest towns. From my early years, I myself was among the traders in counterpoint, and therefore I am speaking from manifold experience. Only we Germans are such fools as to remain with the old jog-trot in many antiquated things and, ridiculously, to want to consider the eyes looking at a sheet of paper to be the point of music, rather than the ears.[28]

Heinichen composed only one opera for the Dresden court theater, *Flavio Crispo*, which was never performed, though it seems possible that the work was completed. The original manuscript by Heinichen is lost; the only extant copy breaks off near the end of the final act. The opera was not performed because of a quarrel between Heinichen and the castratos, Senesino and Berselli, about an aria for Berselli. Allegedly, the quarrel was also the reason why August the Strong dissolved the opera company. But since the prince-elector settled the quarrel before the singers' dismissal, and Alessandro Mauro, the carpenters, and the painters were dismissed as well, August the Strong probably used it to dispose of artists who proved to be too expensive to retain after the wedding celebrations. In the years following, Heinichen wrote secular and sacred music for the court until he died of tuberculosis in 1729.

Heinichen's works show that he was a gifted composer. His contemporaries appreciated his music, though most of it could be heard and performed only in Dresden. Presumably, none of Heinichen's compositions were published in his lifetime because of the old, sixteenth-century rule that a court composer's works, especially those written for solemn occasions, had to remain the sole possession of the sovereign. Only a few manuscript copies of his compositions survived in places other than the Dresden court library. Recently, Heinichen's concertos and his church music have been rediscovered and newly performed, but his major secular vocal works, especially *Diana su l'Elba* and *La Gara degli Dei*, remain unknown to a broader public. Surely, one of the reasons for this is that both manuscripts are difficult to read due to water damage. Another reason is that works like these are too-often believed to have importance relating only to the occasion on which they were performed and to lack inherent musical value. But since both pieces were composed for one of the most famous celebrations of the eighteenth century and because Heinichen had an orchestra and singers of rare quality at his disposal, it is clear that he could demonstrate the full extent of his compositional skills in the two serenate. (August the Strong expected no less; he raised Heinichen's salary by 300 taler after hearing the works.)

Both works exemplify Heinichen's masterful compositional style, which was far more *galant* than the contrapuntal style of the North German Baroque composers and matched perfectly the style of Lotti in Dresden. Harmonically, Heinichen's style is comparatively simple. A typical example is the beginning of Diana's aria, "Mille belve dalle selve" (no. 3), in *Diana su l'Elba* where almost exclusively he employs broken G-major chords, only occasionally and *en passant* using D-major chords between them. This simple harmonic device allows for equally simple and fluent melodies in the singers' parts, many of which consist likewise of broken chords, thus enhancing the harmonic smoothness of the music. Due to his deliberately simple harmonic devices, Heinichen's motives often lack catchy melodic contours. The most distinctive trait in Heinichen's compositions, however, is his use of different tone colors, unusual instrumental combinations, and unusual sonorities that more than once comprise the real musical "motives." Thus, he expanded his predominantly Venetian style and gave the court musicians in Dresden opportunities to demonstrate their virtuosity. This was certainly the case in Heinichen's *Diana su l'Elba* and *La Gara degli Dei*.

Heinichen was also renowned as the author of two theoretical books: *Neu erfundene und gründliche Anweisung . . . zu vollkommener Erlernung des General-Basses* (Hamburg, 1711) and *Der General-Bass in der Composition, oder: Neue und gründliche Anweisung* (Dresden, 1728). Because Heinichen, whom Burney called "the Rameau of Germany," believed that learning thoroughbass accompaniment was the "best method for learning the entire technique of composition,"[29] both of his books treat encyclopedically the compositional practice of his time. *Der General-Bass in der Composition* is much more than an enlarged edition of Heinichen's first book: it gives additional insights into the principles of composition, including Venetian techniques and comments on the realization of an unfigured bass.

Diana su l'Elba

As no poet is mentioned in the sources of *Diana su l'Elba* and *La Gara degli Dei*, Heinichen's two serenate for the wedding festivities, we can only speculate about the author(s). Since Antonio Maria Luchini, the poet commissioned with the Italian singers in 1717, escaped with a young Saxon woman in 1718, Stefano Benedetto Pallavicino, who had been court poet under Elector Johann Georg III, was commissioned in June 1719 to write the libretto of *Teofane* and, presumably, the librettos of *Diana su l'Elba* and *La Gara degli Dei*. However, since the poetic and stylistic levels of the serenate librettos are distinctively different (with *Diana* at a lower level), it is possible that they were written by different poets. It is also possible that the differences between the librettos are due to the fact that *La Gara degli Dei* was the more important piece and thus required a more ambitious text.

As usual in vocal compositions of this kind in the eighteenth century, the text of *Diana su l'Elba* alludes to ancient mythology. Diana was the goddess of the hunt who maintained her virginity and required the same from her retinue of nymphs. In this regard, her behavior was quite the opposite of Venus and Athena, both of whom seduced men with their beauty and with Hera competed for the golden apple, which Paris awarded to Venus, the most beautiful goddess.[30]

The poet, however, chose not to celebrate the bride as allegorical impersonation of Venus (the young couple was not beautiful by any means). Rather, since both the prince-elector and the archduchess were renowned as hunters, the poet exercised caution and denied explicitly the importance of beauty, denouncing Venus as a goddess who made men's minds soft and effeminate and declaring that the most famous heros of all time had sprung from Diana's followers. Climene,[31] the nymph who gave birth to Phaëton (and therefore had disobeyed Diana's rule of chastity), serves to exemplify the damaging effects of the struggle for beauty. According to the nymph Nisa,[32] Climene had looked into the water of a spring in order to comb her hair and beautify herself. Nisa further reports that she saw Climene beating the hounds and avoiding the strains of hunting by avoiding steep hills and going instead to the plains.

Alcippe warns Climene against love (a feeling connected to beauty): if she feels love, she should drown herself in the deepest wave. The music of Alcippe's aria resembles the raging waves of the sea more than those of the river Elbe, which at a first glance seems odd in the context of the serenata. But surely most of the audience knew that according to mythology one of Poseidon's sons had desired Alcippe and raped her. Alcippe, therefore, represents yet another facet of the dangers of beauty. Diana is the appropriate goddess to represent the virtues of the archduchess, for as Daphne[33] says, only the pleasure of hunting makes a heart adore Diana. The goddess of the hunt adds that the archduchess possesses womankind's true virtues, which are not seductiveness but inner beauty and the ability to give birth to new heros.

In her recitative, "Tu, che nel cor mi vedi," Climene alludes to the judgment of Paris: even Athena wanted to be rewarded for her beauty by Paris with the golden apple (*pomo d'oro*), and Venus would compete even with the beauty of Diana. Diana replies that she despises the pride of beauty, thus indirectly referring to the opera *Il pomo d'oro*. In 1668 Antonio Cesti's famous opera *Il pomo d'oro* (libretto by Francesco Sbarra) was performed in Vienna as part of the celebrations for the wedding of Emperor Leopold I and the Infanta Margarita Teresa.[34] At the end of the opera, the golden apple, which according to mythology bore the inscription "for the fairest," was not awarded to Venus (as it had been in mythology). Jupiter himself decided that the apple should be bestowed on the empress because she united the beauty of Venus, the bravery of Juno, and the wisdom of Athena. Beauty alone was not the criterion for winning the golden apple, rather it was the sum of imperial virtues, including bearing new heroes (which was depicted explicitly at the end of *Il pomo d'oro*, when the stage design represented the Habsburg lineage and the anticipated descendants of the newly wed couple).

The golden apple appeared in Vienna in another guise: in an allegorical play set between the acts of a Latin tragedy entitled *Hymenaei de Marte triumphus in Adelhaida Italiae regina Othonis Magni sponsa*,[35] which was performed for the wedding celebrations of Joseph I, son of Emperor Leopold I, and Amalie Wilhelmine of Braunschweig-Lüneburg on 22 April 1699. In the allegorical plot, Diana announced the future birth of many children to the couple (that is, she uttered the same hopes as Diana in *Diana su l'Elba*), and an imperial eagle together with a golden apple appeared, symbolizing the Roman Empire and the house of Habsburg. (This golden apple, however, was picked by Hymenaeus for Jupiter from the garden of the Hesperides. Since the golden apple represented the Habsburg Empire in both cases, its exact mythological origin probably did not matter.)

Therefore, the reference to the apple in *Diana su l'Elba* during the celebrations in Dresden could be understood in a twofold way: as a symbol of the archduchess's future status as mother of heros and as a symbol of the Habsburg Empire. In fact, on the feast of Jupiter in September 1719, the prince-elector carried a shield with a crowned eagle and the inscription "sans crainte" (without fear) and August the Strong carried a shield with a golden apple of brass and the inscription "A la plus belle" (for the fairest), thus referring to Habsburg tradition.[36]

The sonata (no. 1) of *Diana su l'Elba* is typical of early eighteenth-century compositions of this kind, with its two fast movements surrounding a brief adagio movement. After a short introductory chorus (no. 2) and her recitative, Diana begins one of Heinichen's most impressive arias, "Mille belve dalle selve" (no. 3), accompanied by three horns to evoke the hunt. Like almost all of Heinichen's arias, it is in da capo form. The orchestration of Climene's aria, "Così sorgea la Dea de' cori" (no. 4), contrasts with Diana's aria in a manner characteristic of Heinichen: only flutes are used, with an occasional second violin, and the entire aria is at a piano dynamic. Although the dynamics and orchestration seem to suggest a slower tempo, the aria is in a fast tempo (allegro). Climene's coloratura passages on "mar" express the running of the waves. Dafne's aria, "Bella è Cintia" (no. 5), is the first aria in which the oboes double the violins in the ritornello, contrasting with the solo sections in which the accompaniment is reduced to the higher strings and the viola plays the bass (see plate 4).

The audience might have wondered why none of the first three arias were set in a contrasting, slow tempo. The fast tempi of the first arias (especially Diana's) worked to set off in impressive contrast Nisa's aria, "Languido al par del guardo" (no. 6), in which Nisa accuses Climene of being a poor hunter, her arms only weakly flinging her javelin. To paint Climene's weakness, Heinichen composed a slow aria, giving the violins a broken line in measures 7–8 of the ritornello, and utilizing feeble pitch repetitions in the horns, rather than providing the splendid horn parts of Diana's aria. Nevertheless, the "flying" of the spear is painted with coloratura passages, though their fluency is interrupted by a syncopated and more "learned" setting—typical for Heinichen's style on occasion—in measures 22–23 (see also measures 10–11 and 45–48).[37] Alcippe's aria, "Dove profonda più corre l'onda" (no. 7), provides fresh contrast with music that represents the raging and stormy waves of the sea. The use of *unisono* in the aria is a typical feature in compositions for the Dresden court at that time,[38] and Alcippe's octave leaps and broken chords are characteristic of the bass-like arias composed for Vittoria Tesi, the singer who performed the part. Alcippe's advice that Climene should throw herself into the waves if she feels love provides an opportunity for impressive text painting: the downward-moving, stepwise eighth notes mirror the word "scagliati" (throw yourself in) and are followed by coloratura passages that represent the waves (measures 78–92). In Climene's aria, "Questo mio fallo innocente" (no. 8), her weak character is represented with syncopation and chromatic passages as it was in no. 6. *Diana su l'Elba* ends with a chorus (no. 9) that is led by Diana, again accompanied by three horns, who calls the assembly to the hunt. After the chorus, the actual hunt began.

The Horn in Dresden

In 1710 Johann Albert Fischer and Franz Adam Samm were engaged by August the Strong as specialists on the corno da caccia.[39] Lotti and Heinichen were the first composers in Dresden who included the horn in their compositions. Thomas Hiebert gives the four main reasons why they (and subsequent composers) used the horn: "the visual effect of the horn in the orchestra, the programmatic use of the horn to evoke a sense of the hunt, the use of the horn in the capacity of soloist and delineator of structure through the exploitation of the horn's volume and timbral potential, and probably most importantly, the technical prowess of the Dresden horn players."[40]

The use of horns in Lotti's operas and Heinichen's serenate (*Diana su l'Elba, La Gara degli Dei*, and the *Serenata di Moritzburg*, composed for the hunt which followed the wedding celebrations in October 1719) for the wedding festivities may have been an allusion to Habsburg tradition, for horns had been used in operas in Vienna since the beginning of the eighteenth century. In 1718 the Dresden court purchased two Viennese "Waldhörner" with six pairs of crooks that allowed the hornists to play in different keys:

> These horns were likely built by the Leichnambschneider brothers in Vienna. The horns of the Leichnambschneiders were the most advanced in construction at the time: a large bell and a distinct conical bore gave these horns a darker, more robust sound than others of their day. The small-hooped corpus and removable crooks of the Leichnamb-schneiders' horns had the advantage of making possible a comfortable holding position and allowed the basic length of the horns to be altered, unlike the earlier fixed-length large-hooped horns.[41]

Only horns in F were used in Dresden until the 1719 festivities, when Lotti wrote for horns in D in *Teofane*[42] and Heinichen used horns in D, G, and F in his serenate. The two new horns were presumably used in *Diana su l'Elba*, although it is not clear what kind of horn was used for the third horn part. All horn parts in *Diana su l'Elba* are understood to be basso horn parts (that is, sounding below the given pitch).

In *Diana su l'Elba*, one finds some of Heinichen's most impressive writing for the horn. All hornists are required to use the *clarino* register, especially in Diana's aria, "Mille belve dalle selve" (no. 3). At the beginning of the aria (measures 3–4) the first hornist should employ a *messa di voce*, one of the preferred expressive ornaments, with which Diana has to compete in her sustained notes. The pitch b', which is not part of the horn's harmonic series (though it was used quite frequently by Heinichen), appears in the second horn part. The Dresden hornists must have produced the pitch by hand-stopping or "lipping down" from the eighth harmonic (c''). The use of three horns (in nos. 3 and 9) may have been intended to refer to the "Most Illustrious Gathering" (a kind of family summit conference of the elector, his brothers, and their families) of 1678, when the arrival of Diana was announced by three nymphs playing French horns in a procession.[43]

The Singers

Who sang in *Diana su l'Elba*? There are no hints in the manuscript or other sources, but one can make a reasonable guess. First, although August the Strong had specially engaged the Italian castratos for the performance of Italian vocal works, all parts in *Diana su l'Elba* were sung by female singers, as an account of the Prussian Privy Councillor von Posadowsky proves:

> Before the beginning of the hunt a ship built especially for this occasion, the rear of which represented a big mussel, approached the canopy[44] and the Italian female singers ["Sängerinnen"], representing Diana and some naiads, sang a short text while the hunters all went to the stables and forced the game into the water, which consisted of approximately two hundred to three hundred deer and some wild boars and sows.[45]

(See plates 1 and 2.) In September 1719 the following female singers were available in Dresden:

Sopranos: Santa Scarabelli Stella (prima donna), Margherita Durastanti, Livia Costantini, Johanna Elisabeth Hesse, Madeleine du Salvay.[46]

Altos: Coralli (Antonia Maria Novelli Laurenti) and Vittoria Tesi.

Of the four sopranos available,[47] Costantini arguably can be excluded from further consideration because she sang mostly in intermezzi and would not have been cast in one of the major works of September 1719.[48] Assuming that the role of Diana, like that of Giove,[49] was sung by the same singer in two pieces (*Diana su l'Elba* and *La Gara degli Dei*), Diana must be considered the most important female part. Since Santa Stella was the prima donna, she would have taken the leading role. The tessitura of Climene in *Diana su l'Elba* is the same as that of Gismonda in *Teofane*, sung by Durastanti (*Teofane:* e'–a"; *Diana su l'Elba:* e'–a"). Du Salvay may have sung the part of Nisa.

The part of Alcippe must have been sung by Tesi (*Teofane:* g–d"; *Diana su l'Elba:* g–d"). Alcippe's aria (like Marte's two arias in *La Gara degli Dei*) accords with Quantz's description of Tesi's voice and repertoire: "The Tesi was by nature gifted with a strong manly contralto. In the year 1719 she mostly sang arias composed in a bass-like manner."[50] Thus, Coralli must have sung the role of Dafne (*Teofane:* c'–d"; *Diana su l'Elba:* b–d"). The probable cast of *Diana su l'Elba* is the following: Santa Stella (Diana); Durastanti (Climene); Coralli (Dafne); du Salvay (Nisa); and Tesi (Alcippe).

Notes on Performance

In contrast to *La Gara degli Dei*,[51] neither the manuscript of *Diana su l'Elba* (Sächsische Landesbibliothek—Staats- und Universitätsbibliothek Dresden, Musikabteilung, Mus. 2398-L-2) nor the drawing of its performance (see plate 2) suggests the use of a theorbo or second basso continuo group. Possibly, there was too little space on the vessel for a second basso continuo group.

As in *La Gara degli Dei*, both of the oboe parts were played by two oboists apiece. Since the oboists played flute as well, the instrumentation includes four flutes: two recorders (*flauto dolce*) and two transverse flutes. No oboe partbook survives for *Diana su l'Elba*, but according to Dresden performance practice, *colla parte* oboe parts can be assumed unless otherwise specified in the score. (In the sonata [no. 1], measure 58, the oboists presumably substituted c' and b for the last two notes, which fell below their range.)There are some exceptions to this rule, however. In cases when oboes accompany the solo section of an aria, as opposed to the ritornello, only one oboist per part was employed. (Or, as in no. 8, the oboes were tacit in the solo sections.) Further, the oboe parts were tacit when the harpsichord played *tasto solo* (see no. 2). Finally, there exists an ambiguous situation for oboe use in no. 6. Analogously to no. 3, one might assume that Heinichen did not want to use oboes because he used horns. However, since Heinichen did not write the instruction "senza Hautb:" in the manuscript score (D-Dl, Mus. 2398-L-2), the use of *colla parte* oboes in the ritornellos cannot be ruled out.

Notes

1. Nevertheless, after the death of Karl VI in 1740, Friedrich August (II) tried to establish Maria Josepha as Karl's heir through war and formed an alliance with Frederic the Great, who was already at war with Austria, and Karl Albert of Bavaria, who was elected emperor in 1742. The war was not successful; rather, it was the beginning of a chain of military and political disasters that in the long run led to the Prussian bombardment of Dresden in 1760, during which many of the scores in the Dresden court chapel were destroyed by fire. See Wolfgang Horn, *Die Dresdener Hofkirchenmusik 1720–1745: Studien zu ihren Voraussetzungen und ihrem Repertoire* (Kassel, 1987), 26–28.

2. See Michael Walter, "Italienische Musik als Repräsentationskunst der Dresdener Fürstenhochzeit von 1719," in *Elbflorenz*, ed. Barbara Marx (forthcoming).

3. Fiona McLauchlan, "Lotti's *Teofane* (1719) and Handel's *Ottone* (1723): A Textual and Musical Study," *Music & Letters* 78 (1997): 350.

4. See Antonio Lotti, *Duetti, terzetti, e madrigali a più voci*, ed. Thomas Day, Recent Researches in the Music of the Baroque Era, vols. 44–45 (Madison, 1985).

5. See Moritz Fürstenau, *Zur Geschichte der Musik und des Theaters am Hofe der Kurfürsten von Sachsen und Könige von Polen* (Dresden, 1862), 132–33.

6. Jean Baptiste Volumier (Woulmyer) was concertmaster from 1709 to 1728. Johann Georg Pisendel was court violinist beginning in 1712 and concertmaster from 1728 to 1755.

7. Johann Joachim Quantz, "Herrn Johann Joachim Quantzens Lebenslauf, von ihm selbst entworfen," in Friedrich Wilhelm Marpurg, *Historisch-kritische Beyträge zur Aufnahme der Musik* (1755), 1:206–7. Translation in *On Playing the Flute*, by Johann Joachim Quantz, trans. Edward R. Reilly (London, 1966), xiii–xiv.

8. Between 1709 and 1717 no court theater in Dresden existed because the old opera house at the Taschenberg served as Catholic church for the court and the Kleine Komoedien-haus am Zwingerwall, built in 1696–97, had been pulled down in 1709. See Jean Louis Sponsel, *Der Zwinger, die Hoffeste und die Schloßbaupläne zu Dresden* (Dresden, 1924), 235.

9. Earlier performances of *Giove in Argo* and *Ascanio* took place in the Redoutensaal of the palace.

10. See Fürstenau, *Zur Geschichte der Musik und des Theaters*, 151. The purpose of Handel's sojourn on the continent was to look for "a Company of the choicest singers in Europe" that he could engage "for the opera in the Hay-Market" (*Appleby's Weekly Journal*, 21 February 1719, quoted in Johannes Gress, "Händel in Dresden," *Händel-Jahrbuch* 9 [1963]: 135). (From the Dresden company he was able to engage immediately only Margherita Durastanti; other Dresden singers did not join the opera company of the Haymarket theater before September 1720, when they were dismissed by August the Strong.) Presumably, Handel performed one (or several) of his harpsichord pieces at the court; in February 1720 he was paid 100 *Ducaten*—a delay which was not uncommon due to the financial situation of August the Strong. Handel already knew Lotti from his sojourn in Venice and must have been impressed by his music, for he often quoted or alluded to it in his works. His opera *Ottone* was based on the libretto of *Teofane*, and Handel was also author of a *pasticcio* on the libretto of *Giove in Argo*. The purpose of Telemann's journey to Dresden is not explicitly clear (see Johann Mattheson, *Grundlage einer Ehrenpforte* [Hamburg, 1740; reprint, ed. M. Schneider, Berlin, 1910], 364–65), but Telemann certainly knew that during the wedding celebrations he had a good chance to have one or another of his compositions performed and to be paid well for it. He composed a violin concerto in B-flat major ("Concerto grosso per il Sig.ʳ Pisendel"), which bears the date "14. Sept. 1719," written in Telemann's hand. If this is true, the first occasion for a performance of the concerto was the Turkish feast on 17 September. Equally, the so-called "Suitenkonzert" in F major, presumably composed for Pisendel as well, could have been performed on the same occasion. The *polacca* movement would have especially pleased August the Strong and the Polish nobles. The janissary band playing at the Turkish feast was also a Polish band; therefore Telemann's concerto would have matched the Polish "touch" of the feast.

11. See Monika Schlechte, *Kunst der Repräsentation—repräsentative Kunst (Zeremoniell und Fest am Beispiel von Julius Bernhard von Rohrs "Einleitung zur Ceremoniel-Wissenschaft" und der Festlichkeiten am Dresdner Hof im Jahr 1719)* (Habilitations-Schrift, Technische Universität Dresden, 1990), 1:99–100.

12. No. 200 in Gustav Adolph Seibel's catalog of works by Heinichen. Gustav Adolph Seibel, *Das Leben des Königl. Polnischen und Kurfürstl. Sächs. Hofkapellmeisters Johann David Heinichen nebst chronologischem Verzeichnis seiner Opern (mit Angaben über Fundorte, Entstehungsjahre, Aufführungen, Textbuch, Textdichter usw. und thematischem Katalog seiner Werke)* (Leipzig, 1913).

13. No. 201 in Seibel's catalog (ibid.).

14. The original ship served the Venetian doge.

15. August the Strong had to become a Catholic in order to be elected king in Poland, which caused many political problems, for Saxony was the most important Protestant country in the Roman Empire. In 1712 in Bologna his son, Friedrich August, converted to Catholicism, a precondition to marrying the Austrian archduchess and becoming the successor of August the Strong as king in Poland. The court chapel was the only Catholic church in Dresden.

16. See Walter, "Italienische Musik als Repräsentationskunst der Dresdener Fürstenhochzeit von 1719."

17. See note 10.

18. For the tradition of the festivities of the seven planets, see Schlechte, *Kunst der Repräsentation—repräsentative Kunst;* and Ingrid S. Weber, *Planetenfeste Augusts des Starken. Zur Hochzeit des Kronprinzen 1719* (Munich, 1985).

19. Although the libretto of *La Gara degli Dei* refers to "nel Real Giardino del Palazzo detto Chinese," the Dutch palace (bought from Count Flemming by August in 1717 in order to include it in the wedding festivities) was not renamed the Japanese palace before 1732.

20. Helen Watanabe-O'Kelly, *Triumphal Shews: Tournaments at German-speaking Courts in their European Context 1560–1730* (Berlin, 1992), 130–36.

21. Ibid., 132. The Italian term for the festivity was "Carrosello di quattro Elementi." Though the German equivalent of "carrosello" is "Karussell," which may also refer to a carousel, the term "carrosello" was derived from the Roman "curribus solis" or the Italian "carro del sole," i.e., the (magnificent) carriage of the Sun that formed part of a procession. Essentially, a "carossello" was a running at the head (usually a "Turkish" head) or the ring using javelins or lances. The "carossello" was sometimes connected with a horse ballet as was the case in the wedding festivities in 1719.

22. Ibid., 134. "Once all combatants are in position, they attempt to pierce the ring with a lance, hit a target with the javelin and strike a papier machè ball with the sword. Then the spectators are treated to what a contemporary source calls the 'jet de boules,' in which a member of one team chases another, throwing earthenware balls at him, while he attempts to escape, protecting his back with a shield. . . . Once this is over, the king leads all the riders in a curious labyrinthine formation-ride in and out among pyramidal columns dotted round the amphitheatre as supports for various targets" (Ibid., 134–35).

23. See the drawing in *The New Grove Dictionary of Music and Musicians*, s.v. "Dresden," by Ortrun Landemann.

24. In 1709, when the Danish King Frederic IV visited August the Strong in Dresden, Carlo Agostino Badia's serenade *La Pace e Marte supplicanti a vanti al trono della Gloria* was performed on green-decorated ships, illuminated by torches, on the river Elbe before a fireworks display. See Irmgard Becker-Glauch, *Die Bedeutung der Musik für die Dresdener Hoffeste bis in die Zeit Augusts des Starken* (Kassel, 1951), 92–93.

25. Since the sources differ from each other with respect to that festivity, it is not clear whether there really was a cantata. The entry in the *Hof-Journal* (Sächsisches Hauptstaatsarchiv, Oberhofmarschallamt O IV Nr. 100: *Verbesserter und Alter | Schreib=Calender | Vor | Sr. Königl. Majest. in Pohlen | und Churfl. Durchl. zu Sachsen | Churfürsenthum, incorporirt= und an= | dere Lande, | Auf das Jahr Christi | M.DCC.XIX* [Hofjournal 1719], entry of 20 September) reads "vor der Mercerie wurde eine Ita. Comoedie gespielet" and could be the description of a cantata since "comoedie" was often used for "opera" in the entries. On the other hand, it is possible that the *Hof-Journal* confused the supposed cantata with Johann Christoph Schmidt's opera-ballet, *Les quatre saisons.*

26. The mock fairs during festivities in Dresden during the eighteenth century usually imitated the Leipzig fairs.

27. For further details, see *The New Grove Dictionary of Music and Musicians*, s.v. "Heinichen, Johann David," by George J. Buelow; and Horn, *Die Dresdener Hofkirchenmusik 1720–1745.*

28. "Ich gestehe gerne, daß ich vielmahls in tieffes Nachsinnnen gerathen, woher es doch immer kommen müsse, daß es bey unsern Zeiten noch Leuthe gibt, welche die in der Music schon längst verfallenen *rudera antiquitatis* zu erheben, und zu defendiren, suchen? Allein, meines Erachtens, seynd dieses wohl die wichtigsten Ursachen davon: denn erstlich haben solche musicalische Herren *Antiquarii* ihre gantze Jugend, oder vielmehr ihre gantze Lebens Zeit mit solchen Grillen zugebracht, und das wollen sie bey Leibe nicht umsonst gelernet haben. Ja, weil es nunmehro ohne dis zu

langsam wäre, der Sache weiter nachzudenken, so ergehet es ihnen hierinnen *agreablement* wie denen Gottseeligen Müttern, welche nur diejenigen Kinder am liebsten haben, die ihnen der Geburth am sauersten worden. *Pro secundo*, so scheinen es solchen in *praejudiciis* steckenden Leuthen lauter Böhmische Dörfer zu seyn, wenn man heute zu Tage saget, daß zu einer *touchanten* Ohren-Music vielmehr subtile und geschickte Regeln, nebst einer langwierigen *Praxi*, gehören, als zu einer Herz-druckenden Augen-Music, welche auf dem unschuldigen Papier, nach allen *venerablen Contrapuncten* der Herren *Cantors* in den allerklernesten Städlein, buchmartirisiret worden. Ich habe mich von Jugend auf selbst unter der Zahl der Contrapuncts-Händler befunden: und also rede ich alles aus vielfältiger Erfahrung. Und wir Teutschen allein seynd solche Narren, daß wir, in vielen abgeschmackten Dingen, lieber bey dem alten Schlendrian bleiben, und lächerlicher weise mehr die Augen auf das Papier, als die Ohren, zum *objecto* der Music machen wollen." Heinichen to Johann Mattheson, Dresden, 7 December 1717, quoted in Johann Mattheson, *Critica Musica*, 212–13.

29. *The New Grove Dictionary of Music and Musicians*, s.v. "Heinichen."

30. During the wedding of Peleus and Thetis, a golden apple bearing the inscription "for the fairest" was thrown amongst the guests by Eris, the goddess of strife. Paris was to judge in the competition and to award the golden apple to one of the goddesses. He bestowed the apple on Venus, who promised him the love of the most beautiful women as reward. According to the myth, the event was the starting point for the Trojan war.

31. The daughter of Ocean and Tethys, Clymene was married to the Egyptian king Merops; Helios was Phaeton's father.

32. The personification of Mount Nysa, the boeotian nymph Nysa was supposed to have reared Bacchus.

33. The nymph Daphne was daughter of the river Peneios.

34. See Marc Antonio Cesti, *Il Pomo d'Oro. Bühnenfestspiel. Prolog und erster Akt,* ed. Guido Adler (1896; reprint Graz, 1959), xiv; Antonio Cesti, *Il pomo d'oro (Music for Acts III and V from Modena, Biblioteca Estense, Ms. Mus. E. 120)*, ed. Carl B. Schmidt, Recent Researches in the Music of the Baroque Era, vol. 42 (Madison, 1982); and Walter, "Italienische Musik als Repräsentationskunst der Dresdener Fürstenhochzeit von 1719."

35. The plot of the tragedy was based on Antonio Draghi's opera *L'Adalberto, overo La Forza dell'astuzie Femminile*. The plot of *Teofane* mirrors the plot of *L'Adalberto*. Both Draghi's opera and the Latin tragedy were certainly known at the court of Dresden.

36. Schlechte, "Recueil des dessins et gravures representent les solemnites du mariages: Das Dresdner Fest von 1719 im Bild," in *Image et spectacle. Actes du XXXIIe Colloque International d'Etudes Humanistes du Centre d'Etudes Supérieures de la Renaissance (Tours, 29 juin–8 juillet 1989)*, ed. Pierre Béhar, Chloe: Beihefte zu Daphnis 15 (Amsterdam, 1993), 147.

37. While the completed version uses two horns and non-pizzicato strings, an uncompleted version of Nisa's aria, with flutes, two horns, and pizzicato strings (including *violoni pizzicati*), survives in the manuscript of *Diana su l'Elba* (see plate 5).

38. Heinichen also employed the technique in *La Gara degli Dei* and *Flavio Crispo*. Francesco Maria Veracini wrote a complete movement in *unisono* in one of his overtures composed for the prince-elector in Venice in 1716.

39. See Thomas Hiebert, "The Horn in Early Eighteenth Century Dresden: The Players and their Repertory" (D.M.A. diss., University of Wisconsin, Madison, 1989).

40. Ibid., 14.

41. Ibid., 54.

42. Hiebert believed erroneously that there are parts for horns in C in the Naiad's aria at the end of act 2 of *Teofane*. However, he overlooked the notice "Un tuon più Alto" above the basso part, which clearly meant that the complete aria had to be transposed up a whole step, not the bass part alone. Therefore the Naiad's aria is in D major rather than C major,

and the horns used were horns in D. See the score of *Teofane* (D-Dl, Mus. 2159-F-7), 312. Herbert Heyde suggested incorrectly that a horn in C alto was used for the Naiad's aria, in his article "Blasinstrumente und Bläser der Dresdener Hofkapelle in der Zeit des Fux-Schülers Johann Dismas Zelenka (1710–1745)," in *J. J. Fux und die barocke Bläsertradition. Kongreß-Bericht Graz 1985*, ed. B. Habla, Alta Musica 9 (Tutzing, 1987), 59. Regarding the horns, Heyde's article is beset with mistakes and is not reliable.

43. Wantanabe-O'Kelly, *Triumphal Shews*, 111.

44. The canopy was for the elector/king, his wife, the prince-elector, and his wife. The drawing of *Diana su l'Elba* in *The New Grove Dictionary of Music and Musicians*, s.v. "Dresden," shows only the right half of the picture, which at some point was divided into two halves. Consequently, the left half of the canopy is missing in the reproduction (see plates 1 and 2).

45. "Vor Anfang der Jagt näherte sich ein besonders hierzu erbautes Schiff, dessen Hintertheil eine große Muschel vorstellte, gegen ermeldeten Schirm, und wurde von denen darauf placirten italienischen Sängerinnen unter dem Namen der Diane und einiger Najaden eine kurze Poesie abgesungen, mittler Zeit sich die gantze Jägerey in die Bestallung verfüget und das Wild, so etwan in zwei biß dreihundert Stück Rothwild und einigen wilden Schweinen bestunde, in das Wasser forciret." Quoted in Paul Haake, *Christiane Eberhardine und August der Starke: Eine Ehetragödie* (Dresden, 1930), 156.

46. The names of Johanna Elisabeth Hesse and Madeleine du Salvay are given in this volume as they appear in Dresden sources; however, articles on these singers may be found in *The New Grove Dictionary of Music and Musicians* under "Johanna Elisabeth Döbricht" and "Maria Maddalena Salvai," respectively.

47. Since Quantz mentions Hesse only as a singer in operas, which must have been *Giove in Argo* and *Ascanio*, it is improbable that she sang in *Diana su l'Elba*. Quantz, "Herrn Johann Joachim Quantzens Lebenslauf," 112.

48. Costantini did not sing in *Ascanio* in 1718 and only sang the minor role of Vespetta in *Giove in Argo* in 1717.

49. Giuseppe Maria Boschi (bass) sang the part of Giove in *La Gara degli Dei* and also the part of Giove in the cantata *Li quattro elementi*, preceding the Caroussel of the Four Elements on Friday, 15 September. The interconnection of the festivities of the planets considered, it seems probable that it was an intentional decision, possibly by August the Strong himself, to have the same singers perform the same roles in different pieces.

50. "Die Tesi war von der Natur mit einer männlich starken Contraltstimme begabet. Im Jahr 1719 zu Dresden sang sie mehrenteils solche Arien, als man für Bassisten zu setzen pfleget." Quantz, "Herrn Johann Joachim Quantzens Lebenslauf," 227.

51. See Walter, introduction to *La Gara degli Dei*, by Johann David Heinichen, ed. Michael Walter, Recent Researches in the Music of the Baroque Era, vol. 102 (Madison, 2000), xvii.

Text and Translation

The source of the Italian text is the libretto printed in Dresden by J. C. Stössel in 1719. (The copy in the Sächsische Landesbibliothek—Staats- und Universitätsbibliothek Dresden, Hist. Sax. C 1056, 4ᴾ has been used for the edition.) Text not included in the original libretto, but found in the score has been placed in brackets. In preparing the edition, the Italian spelling has been modernized. Accents, apostrophes, capitalization, and punctuation have been changed to conform to modern usage. In the English translation, the recitatives have been translated to clarify sense of entire sentences while the arias have been translated to their line-by-line meaning (even at the expense of natural English discourse).

Diana su l'Elba

Introduzione musicale alla gran caccia fatta sull'acqua nelle vicinanze di Dresda per ordine di S. M. in ocassione delle nozze di L. L. A. A. R. R. (1719)

Si vedrà scendere a seconda del fiume gran macchina, che figura il carro di Diana sostenuto à galla dalle ninfe di detto fiume. Diana. Climene. Dafne. Nisa. Alcippe.

CORO

Alto suono di trombe ritorte
Sfidi a morte—d'intorno le fere;
E dall' onda le naiadi sorte
Siano a parte del nostro piacere.

DIANA

Dolce soggiorno mio verdi foreste,
Per questo dì soffrite,
Ch'io v'abbandoni, e che fendendo il dorso
Del chiaro fiume, a cui diè l'Elba il nome,
Cangino al carro avvinte
Le mie rapide cerve in nuoto il corso.
Qui, dove suole alla squamosa greggia
Tendere il pescator le reti, e gli ami,
Fia, che nascer si veggia
Novo di caccia insolito costume;
E di spoglie, e trofei
Ornamento s'aggiunga a' templi miei.

Mille belve—dalle selve
Qui a cader liete verranno;
Perch'è tal la man, che impiaga,
Che la gloria della piaga
Del morir compensa il danno.

Diana on the Elbe

Musical introduction to the grand aquatic hunt in the vicinity of Dresden by decree of his royal highness on the occasion of the marriage of L. L. A. A. R. R. (1719)

One will see a big machine coming down the river that represents the carriage of Diana kept afloat by nymphs of said river. Diana. Climene. Dafne. Nisa. Alcippe.

CHORUS

Loud sound of horns
challenge to death amidst the beasts;
and naiads come from beneath the wave
to join our pleasure.

DIANA

Green forests of my sweet sojourn, today you have to endure that I leave you. Dividing the back of the clear river, which has been named Elbe, my swift hinds bound to the carriage will change their running to swimming. Here, where the fisherman used to cast his nets and his fish-hooks for the scaly flock, it shall be that one will see a new, unusual kind of hunting. And mounted animals and trophies will be added as ornaments to my temple.

Thousand beasts of the forest
will be happy to fall here;
because the hand wounding them is of such a kind
that the wound's glory
will make up for dying.

CLIMENE

O qual d'argenteo lume
Al tuo apparir, o diva
Tutto risplende il fiume,
E si copre di fior l'opposta riva!
Ei si diria, che quelle
Son di Cipro le spiaggie, e che dall'acque
Con miracol novello
Il mondo a innamorar Venere nacque.

Così sorgea
La dea de' cori
Di grembo al mar;
E cento Grazie,
E cento Amori
Con Citerea
Nasceano al par.

DAFNE

Ingiurioso è il paragon, Climene,
Se tu eguagli a Diana
La madre di Cupido
Fatta signora, e dea da gente vana,
Una gli animi forti
Rende sovente effeminati, e molli;
L'altra d'ozio nemica
Ai rischi, alla fatica
Tempra le menti; e dai seguaci suoi
Trasse ogni etade i più famosi eroi.

Bella è Cintia; ma il suo aspetto
Non inspira—a chi la mira
Vane idee di folle amor.
Sol di nobile diletto,
Che a virtù non vien conteso,
Fa ch'è preso—un gentil cor.

NISA

Di Venere, e d'Amor sì ben ragioni,
Cara Climene mia,
Che ti rendon sospetta i tuoi sermoni.
Or mi rimembra: io ti mirai sovente,
Onde compor sovra la fronte il crine,
Consigliarti col fonte,
E del fresco mattin temer le brine.
Ti vidi sì, ti vidi
Trar lenti i passi in caccia,
Gl'erti colli schivar, cercar i piani,
E abbondonar la traccia,
E senza colpa aver in ira i cani.
Che si, ch'altro piacer di se t'invoglia,
Ond'abbi poi e pentimento, e doglia.

Languido al par del guardo
Vibra il tuo braccio il dardo
Qualor prende a ferir;
Ne punto ai del valore,
Che dee sentir nel core
Chi Cintia vuol seguir.

CLYMENE

When you appear, O goddess, the river shines like a silvery light and the opposite bank is covered with flowers [the prince-elector and the archduchess]! One will say that these are the shores of Cyprus [Venus's birthplace] and that, due to a new miracle, Venus was born out of the water in order to enchant the world.

Thus came into being
the goddess of the northwest winds
out of the sea's womb;
and a hundred Graces
and a hundred Cupids
with Cytherea [Venus]
have been born likewise.

DAPHNE

Offensive is the comparison, Clymene, if you equate Diana to the mother of Cupid, who has been made lady and goddess of people of no use, and who often has made effeminate and soft the brave [male] minds, whereas the other [Diana] as a foe to idleness strengthens minds for risks and difficulties. And from her followers arose in every epoch the most famous heros.

Cynthia [Diana] is beautiful, but her appearance
does not inspire in the one who looks at her
vain notions of love's delusion.
Only the noble delight [the hunt],
which does not contend with virtue,
lets her win a noble heart.

NYSA

My dear Clymene, you are speaking so reasonably about Venus and Cupid that your speeches arouse suspicion. Now I remember: I often watched you fearing the hoarfrost of the fresh morning and looking for advice from the spring [using it as a mirror] in order to arrange your hair upon your brow. I saw you, yes, I saw you pacing slowly during the hunt, evading the steep hills, looking for the plains, leaving the track, and bringing the hounds to ire without their fault [beating the hounds]. If anybody stirred you up to another delight, you would have only pain and repentance [you would come into conflict with Diana].

As feeble as your gaze
you brandish your javelin
about to strike;
you do not have a spark of valor,
such as those goddesses feel in their hearts
who are willing to follow Cynthia.

ALCIPPE

Se lo credessi, o Nisa, io qui vorrei
Della faretra mia
Tutte l'arme versar nel sen di lei.
Nè irritato dall'asta, e dalla voce
Torvo cignal feroce
Infuria sì, com'io di sdegno avvampo.
Al solo udir di que' profani nomi;
Nè vittima più grata
A Diana oltraggiata
Offerirsi potria d'un cor infido,
Che tradisse in segreto
Gli altari suoi per incensar Cupido.

    Dove profonda
    Più corre l'onda,
    Se senti amore in sen, scagliati, e mori.
    E fa che in lei tu spenga, in lei nasconda
    L'illecite tue fiamme, i tuoi rossori.

CLIMENE

Tu, che nel cor mi vedi,
Vergine dea ben sai,
Se contro te peccai.
O lassa me! se a un falso zel tu credi.
Pregio darti di bella
Dunque fu sì gran colpa? e in riva al Xanto
Forse Pallade anch'ella
Non aspirò della bellezza al vanto?
Nè di vittoria andria Ciprigna altera,
Se tu del pomo d'oro
Scender degnavi a contrastar con loro.

DIANA

Non più, Climene errasti; e da tant'anni
Ancella mia saper dovresti omai,
Che vanto di beltate aborro, e sdegno;
Ma da pena ti salvi un dì sì lieto,
In cui di Cintia è tutto festa il regno.

CLIMENE

    Questo mio fallo innocente,
    Dea clemente—ammenderò,
    E taluna, che in me crede
    Poco zelo, e poca fede
    A mentir condannerò.

DIANA

Oggi il tuo zel di segnalar ai campo;
E voi l'ingegno a prova
Tutto volgete ai destinati uffici.
Nè domando a voi già piacer volgari;
Dell'Imeneo beato,
Che il Sangue d'Austria, e di Sassonia accopia,
Penetrò le foreste il lieto grido;
Ecco la Regal Coppia, ecco a qual lume.
S'illustra è riva, e fiume;
E a lei porger diletto oggi è mia sorte.
Nè l'augusto consorte
E ignoto a me, che cento volte il vidi

ALCIPPE

If I believed that, O Nysa, I would want to shoot into her chest all arrows of my quiver. And no ominous and fierce boar is as infuriated by the spear and the hunting calls as I am enraged by scorn, solely hearing those profane names [the names of Venus and Cupid]. And there will be no sacrifice sufficient for the outraged Diana to be offered by a heart which secretly betrayed her altars by flattering Cupid.

    In the depths where
    the deepest wave runs,
    If you feel love in your breast, plunge in and die.
    And in it let extinguish and conceal
    The forbidden flames and your blushes.

CLYMENE

You, who are able to look into my heart, virgin goddess, you know well whether I have sinned against you. Oh poor me, if you believe in [my] false zeal. Was it such a great fault to give you the merit of beauty? And did not Pallas [Athena] herself strive for the glory of beauty [in the contest of the golden apple] on the bank of the river Scamander [near Troy]? And would not even the eminent Kypris [Venus] strive for another victory, if you were worthy to pick the golden apple and to contend for it with them [Hera, Athena, and Venus].

DIANA

Not any more, Clymene, you have erred. Being my maid for many years, you must have known that I detest and despise the pride of beauty. But you are saved from punishment due to such a happy day when all are celebrating Cynthia's kingdom.

CLYMENE

    For my innocent error,
    Merciful goddess, I will amend,
    And that one who believes I have
    little zeal and faith,
    she will be condemned as lying.

DIANA

Today you may show your zeal at the hunt. And you [others] turn to your assigned duties to prove your talent. It is not vulgar pleasures I demand from you. The forests are imbued with the happy call of the wedding, which will unite the blood of Austria and Saxony. Here is the royal couple, here is their beaming light, which illuminates the bank and the river, and today it is my fortune to give the couple the opportunity for pleasure. The illustrious husband is not unknown to me. I saw him hundreds of times as lover of the hunt before sunrise. [I approved the] giving of the heart of this modest youth to the sublime woman for I saw in her that virtue,

Di Caccia amante prevenir l'aurora;
E se alla donna eccelsa
Del severo garzone il cor cedei,
Fu perchè scorsi in lei
Virtù, che il sesso onora,
E con vera beltà gli animi alletta;
Nè del mondo alla speme oppor mi volli,
Che novi eroi da si bel nodo aspetta.

   Su snidate—su forzate
   Le ramose—fere ascose
   A lasciar le verdi sponde;
   E al colpir delle maestre
   Regie destre
   Trovin morte in mezzo all'onde.

CORO

   Su snidate—su forzate
   Le ramose—fere ascose
   A lasciar le verdi sponde;
   Risvegliato al suono, al grido
   Già dal lido
   In più lati ecco risponde.

Segue la Caccia.

which honors the [female] sex, and attracts minds with real beauty. Additionally, I did not want to oppose the hopes of the world, which expects new heros to arise from this beautiful union.

Let's drive out and force
the hidden beasts
to leave the banks, branched and green;
from the hits of the masterly
royal couple
They shall find death amidst the waves.

CHORUS

Let's drive out and force
the hidden beasts
to leave the banks, branched and green;
awaken by the sound and the call
from the shore
from everywhere it resonates.

The hunt follows.

Plate 1. Zacharias Longuelune, performance of *Diana su l'Elba*, pen and ink drawing. Courtesy of Sächsische Landesbibliothek—Staats- und Universitätsbibliothek Dresden, Kupferstich-Kabinett.

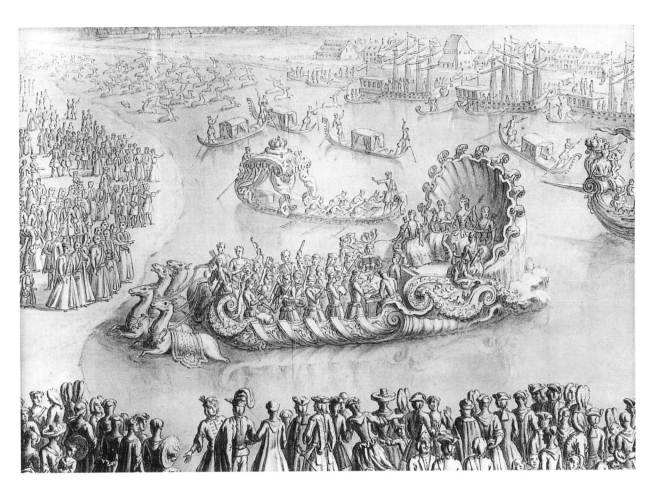

Plate 2. Zacharias Longuelune, performance of *Diana su l'Elba* (detail), pen and ink drawing. Courtesy of Sächsische Landesbibliothek—Staats- und Universitätsbibliothek Dresden, Kupferstich-Kabinett.

Plate 3. Johann David Heinichen, *Diana su l'Elba*, opening page of Climene's aria, "Così sorgea la Dea de' cori" (no. 4). Courtesy of Sächsische Landesbibliothek—Staats- und Universitätsbibliothek Dresden, Musikabteilung, Mus. 2398-L-2.

Plate 4. Johann David Heinichen, *Diana su l'Elba,* opening page of Dafne's aria, "Bella è Cintia" (no. 5). Courtesy of Sächsische Landesbibliothek—Staats- und Universitätsbibliothek Dresden, Musikabteilung, Mus. 2398-L-2.

Plate 5. Johann David Heinichen, *Diana su l'Elba*, opening page of unfinished version of Nisa's aria, "Languido al par del guardo" (no. 6). Courtesy of Sächsische Landesbibliothek—Staats- und Universitätsbibliothek Dresden, Musikabteilung, Mus. 2398-L-2.

Diana su l'Elba

CAST

Diana (Di.) . . . . Soprano
Climene (Cli.) . . . . .Soprano
Dafne (Daf.) . . . . .Alto
Nisa (Ni.) . . . . .Soprano
Alcippe (Al.) . . . . .Alto
Coro (SATB) . . . . Soprano, Alto, Tenor, Bass

ORCHESTRA

3 Corni da caccia (Cn.)
4 Oboi (Ob.)
4 Flauti [2 flauti traversi and 2 flauti dolci played by the oboists] (Fl.)
Violini (Vn.) 1, 2
Viole (Va.)
Bassi [violoncellos, double basses] (B.)
Basso continuo [bassoon, violoncello, double bass, harpsichord] (B.c.)

No. 1. Sonata

Allegro e sempre piano

No. 2. Coro

Al- to   suo- no __ di __

Al- to   suo- no di

Al- to   suo- no di

Al- to   suo- no di

fe- re, __ d'in- tor- no le fe- re. E dal- l'on-da __ le __ na- ia- di

fe- re, __ d'in- tor- no le fe- re. E dal- l'on-da __ le __ na- ia- di

fe- re, __ d'in- tor- no le fe- re. E dal- l'on-da __ le na- ia- di

fe- re, __ d'in- tor- no le fe- re. E dal- l'on-da le na- ia- di

22

Recitative

DIANA

Dol- ce sog-gior-no mi- o ver-di fo- re- ste, per que-sto dì sof- fri- te, ch'io v'ab-ban-don- ni,

e che fen-den- do il dor- so del chia- ro fiu- me, a cui diè l'El- ba il no- me, can- gi-no al car- ro av-

-vin- te le mie ra- pi-de cer- ve in nuo- to il cor- so. Qui, do- ve

suo- le al- la squa-mo-sa greg- gia ten-de-re il pes- ca- tor le re- ti, e gli a- mi, fia,

che na- scer si veg- gia no- vo di cac- cia in- so- li-to co- stu- me; e di spo- glie, e

tro- fei or- na-men- to s'ag- giun- ga a' tem- pli mi- ei.

No. 3. Aria

lie- te ver-

-ran- no,   a ca- der

lie- te _____ ver- ran- no.

[Fine]

Da capo

Recitative

CLIMENE

O qual d'ar-gen- te- o lu- me al tuo ap-pa-rir, o Di- va[,] tut- to ri-splen-de il fiu- me, e si co- pre di fior l'op-po- sta ri- va! Ei si di- ri- a, che quel-le son di Ci- pro le spiag- gie, e che dal- l'ac- que con mi- ra- col no- -vel- lo il mon-do a in- na- mo- rar Ve- ne- re nac- que.

No. 4. Aria

Co- sì ___ sor- ge- a ___ la ___ de- a de'

[divisi]

co- ri ___ di ___ grem- bo al mar, _____

di grem-bo al mar.

Co- sì sor-

-ge- a la de-a de' co-ri __ di grem-bo al mar, __ di grem-bo al mar.

[Fine]

-mo- ri con Ci- te- re- a na- sce- a- no al par, _____

na- scea- no al par.

Da capo

Recitative

DAFNE

In- giu- rio- se è il pa- ra- gon, Cli- me- ne, se tu e- gua- gli a Dia- na la

ma- dre di Cu- pi- do fat- ta si- gno- ra, e de- a da gen- te va- na.

U- na gli a- ni- mi for- ti ren- de so- ven- te ef- fe- mi- na- ti e mol- li;

l'al- tra d'o- zio ne- mi- ca ai ri- schi, al- la fa- ti- ca tem- pra le men- ti; e dai se- gua- ci

su- oi tras- se o- gni e- ta- de i più fa- mo- si e- roi.

No. 5. Aria

fol- le a- mor, _____ di fol- le a- mor.

Bel- la è Cin- tia; ma il

[Fine]

Da capo

Recitative

NISA

Di Ve- ne-re, e d'A- mor sì ben ra- gio- ni, ca- ra Cli-me- ne mi- a, che ti ren-don so-spet- ta

i tuoi ser-mo- ni. Or mi ri-mem-bra: io ti mi-rai so-ven- te, on- de com-por so- vra la fron-te il

cri- ne, con-si-gliar- ti col fon- te, e del fres-co mat- tin te-mer le bri- ne. Ti vi- di, ti vi- di trar

len- ti i pas- si in ca- cia, gl'er- ti col- li schi-var, cer-car i pia- ni, e ab- ban- do-nar la

trac- cia, e sen-za col- pa a- ver in i- ra i ca- ni. Che si, ch'al- tro pia-

-cer di se t'in- vo- glia, on-d'ab-bi poi e pen- ti- men- to, e do- glia.

48

No. 6. Aria

Lan- gui- do al par del guar- do

vi- bra _ il tuo brac- cio il dar- do, vi- bra il __ tuo brac- cio il

dar- - - do qua- lor _ pren- de a fe-

lan gui- do ____ il dar- - - - do

qua- lor _ pren- de a fe- rir.

pun- to ai del va- lo- re, che _ dee sen- tir _ nel _ co- re chi _ Cin- tia vuol se- guir. Ne

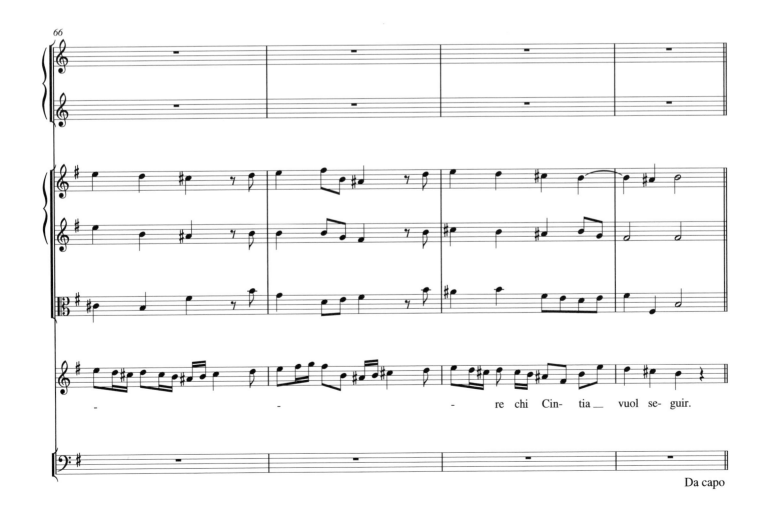

Da capo

56

Recitative

No. 7. Aria

[Fine]

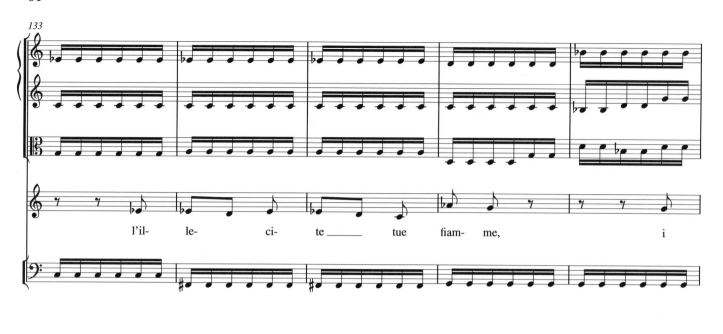

l'il- le- ci- te _____ tue fiam- me, i tuo- i ros- so- ri.

Da capo

Recitative

CLIMENE

Tu, che nel cor mi ve- di, ver- gi- ne de- a ben sa- i, se con- tro a te pec- cai.

O las- sa me! se a un fal- so zel tu cre- di. Pre- gio dar- ti di bel- la dun- que

fu sì gran col- pa? E in ri- va al Xan- to for- se Pal- la- de an- ch'el- la non as- pi- rò

del- la bel- lez- za al van- to? Nè di vit- to- ri- a an- dria Ci- pri- gna al- te- ra, se tu del po- mo

DIANA

d'o- ro scen- der de- gna- vi a con- tra- star con lo- ro. Non più, Cli- me- ne er- ra- sti; e da tan-

-t'an- ni an- cel- la mi- a sa- per do- vre- sti o- mai, che van- to di bel- ta- te ab- bor- ro, e sde- gno; ma da

pe- na ti sal- vi un dì sì lie- to, in cui di Cin- tia è tu- to fe- sta il re- gno.

No. 8. Aria

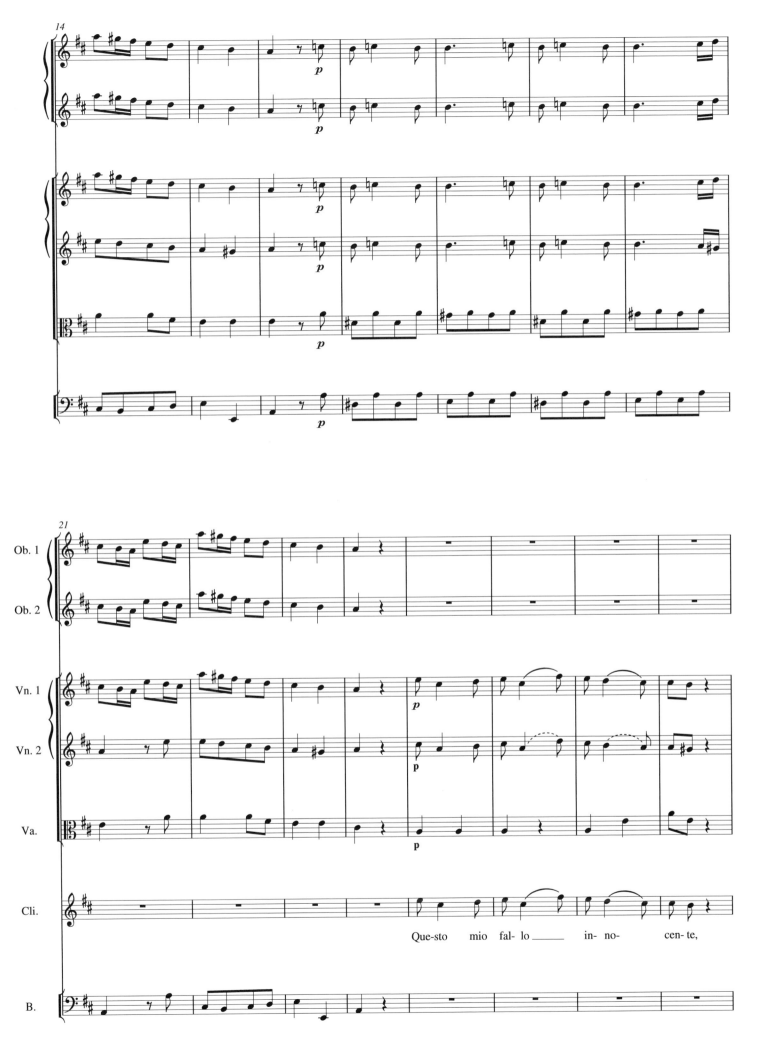

Que-sto   mio   fal- lo _____ in- no-   cen- te,

[Fine]

Vn. 1

Vn. 2

Va.

Cli.

E ta- lu- na, _____ che in me cre- de po- co _____ ze- lo, e _____ po- ca

B.

fe- de a men- tir con- dan- ne- rò, _____

Recitative

72

-cop- pia, pe- ne- trò le fo- re- ste il lie- to gri- do; ec- co la re- gal Cop- pia,

ec- co a qual lu- me. S'il- lu- stra è ri- va, e fiu- me; e a lei por- ger di- let- to og-gi è mia

sor- te. Nè l'au- gu- sto con- sor- te è ig- no- to a me, che cen-to vol-te il vi- di di cac-cia a-man- te

pre- ve- nir l'au- ro- ra; e se al-la don-na ec-cel- sa del se- ve- ro gar-zo- ne il cor ce-

-de- i, fu per-chè scor- si in lei vir- tù, che il ses-so o o- no- ra, e con ve- ra bel-

-tà gli a- ni- mi al- let- ta; nè del mon- do al- la spe- me op-por mi vol- li,

che no- vi e- ro- i da si bel no- do a-spet- ta.

No. 9. Coro

a ___ la- sciar le ___ ver- di spon- de, ___ a la- sciar le ___ ver- di

-sciar le _____ ver- di spon- - de.

-sciar le _____ ver- di spon- - de.

-sciar ___ le ver- di spon- - de.

-sciar ___ le ver- di spon- - de.

-sciar le ver- di spon- - de.

[Fine]

E al col- pir _____ del- le mae- stre re- gie de- stre tro- vin

104

li- do   in   più _____ la- ti   ec- co   ris- pon- de.

li- do   in   più _____ la- ti   ec- co   ris- pon- de.

li- do   in _____ più la- ti   ec- co   ris- pon- de.

li- do   in   più la- ti   ec- co   ris- pon- de.

li- do   in _____ più la- ti   ec- co   ris- pon- de.

Da capo

Critical Report

Sources

The main source for the edition of *Diana su l'Elba* is Heinichen's own handwritten manuscript which is preserved in the Sächsische Landesbibliothek—Staats- und Universitätsbibliothek Dresden, Musikabteilung, (D-Dl, Mus. 2398-L-2) and will hereafter be referred to as *D*. On the title page Heinichen wrote: "Serenata | fatta | su l'Elba | Mes. Settembr. 1719 | di | Heinichen." A stamp of the Königliche Bibliothek was added later, as well as the handwritten remark "vide Textbücher 201." The numbers of the individual pieces are written in red ink; it is not clear whether Heinichen or a copyist wrote them. The manuscript has been damaged by water. Additionally, there are three original partbooks (D-Dl, Mus. 2398-L-2a) for the first violin, second violin ("Violino"), and the viola ("Alto Viola"). The partbooks were especially useful in cases when *D* was barely legible. Heinichen's manuscript measures 22.0 × 28.2 cm in oblong format (ten staves per page) and has been written on paper made by a Dresden mill. The partbooks, written by a copyist, measure 23.3 × 31.5 cm in oblong format (ten staves per page) and likewise have been written on Dresden paper.

A further source for the text is the printed libretto; the title page reads: "Diana su l'Elba | Introduzione Musicale | alla Gran Caccia | fatta sull'Acqua nelle vicinanze di Dresda | di | S. M. | in ocassione delle Nozze | di L. L. A. A. R. R | | Diane sur l'Elbe, | divertissement en Musique pour servir | d'introduction | à la Chasse donnèe sur l'Elbe | par | S. M. | à l'occasion du Mariage | de L. L. A. A. R. R., Dresden: J. C. Stössel [1719]." (The copy in D-Dl, Hist. Sax. C 1056, 4P has been used for the edition.) A manuscript copy of the libretto is incorporated in the "Relation | des Festes de Saxe | que le Roy de Pologne | Auguste II. | de glorieuse memoire | a donné à l'occasion du mariage du Pr: Roy: | Frederic August | son fils unique à present Roy de Pologne |Auguste III. | avec la Serenissime Archiduchesse | Maria Josepha | à present Reine de Pologne Fille de L'Empereur | Ioseph I. | de glorieuse memoire | sous le Nom de 7. Planetes | à Dresde l'Année 1719" (Staatsbibliothek zu Berlin Preussischer Kulturbesitz, ms. germ. fol. 304), which gives a full account of the wedding festivities.

Editorial Methods

This edition of *Diana su l'Elba* is based on *D*. The underlaid Italian text in *D* has been corrected according to the printed libretto. Differences between *D* and the printed libretto that were the result of Heinichen's obviously fast writing as well as orthographical variants have been corrected without comment. Capitalization has been normalized in the underlaid text of the edition.

The movements are numbered according to *D* and the partbooks. The genre designations "Aria" and "Recitative" have been supplied by the editor and do not appear in the original. Since there are no numbers for the recitatives in the sources, they do not have numbers in the edition, although their measures are counted separately from the numbered pieces. In most cases, Heinichen did not indicate instrumentation in front of the staff systems; however, instrumentation is unequivocal because of score order and additional instrumental indications in *D* (see the critical notes for no. 6). Editorial additions concerning instrumentation are enclosed within brackets if the meaning of *D* is uncertain. For the viola part, Heinichen did not write "Alto Viola," as in the partbook, but "Violetta." The indication "Corni da caccia" for the horns in G is found in *D*. All horn parts are understood to be basso horn parts. In the basso continuo, the end of a "tasto solo" section is indicated by an asterisk placed above the last note.

The beaming in the vocal parts has been modernized in cases where it seemed to be appropriate. Original slurring has been retained in vocal melismas because they indicate a true legato, whereas other notes could be sung as *canto granito*. The text distribution, which is not always clear, has been adjusted where necessary without comment. No key signature at the beginning of a number was altered, even if *D* differed from the partbooks (this will be reported in the critical notes). In the edition, accidentals have been repeated after each barline without comment; redundant accidentals have been removed, unless it seemed reasonable to retain them; and cancellation signs have been added without comment, according to modern convention.

Score order has been modernized without comment. If at any place *D* contains hints of separate parts for the winds and brass or if three horn parts were notated in two staves, the parts have been scored separately in the edition. This policy has also been adopted in cases where a negative indication (e.g., "senza Hautb.") makes clear the use of those instruments in the number as a whole. Since the flutes, parts for which are found in the oboe partbooks for *La Gara degli Dei*, were played alternately with the oboes by the same performers, the indication "Flauto traverso, Flauto dolce" excludes the *colla parte* use of oboes. Dynamic indications in *colla parte* voices have been taken over from the violin parts without comment. In the cori (no. 2 and no. 9), the use of *colla parte* oboes is not indicated in *D*, presumably because their use was obvious according to the Dresden performance practice.

Heinichen wrote dynamic indications for instruments in two parts (violins, oboes, horns) between the staves. In the edition those indications are printed separately under the single voices without comment. If forte or piano dynamics have been added by the editor, those indications are printed in roman type, whereas forte and piano dynamics found only in the partbooks are printed in italics with a reference in the critical notes. The same policy is used in respect to slurs and articulation signs found in the partbooks. Slurs added editorially are dashed. Editorial additions, other than dynamics and slurs, are enclosed within square brackets.

Critical Notes

The critical notes document all discrepancies between the edition and *D*, additional remarks by Heinichen, and discrepancies with *D* and additional information in the partbooks. The Helmholtz system of pitch identification in which c' = middle C is used. The following abbreviations are used: M(m). = measure(s), *D* = Heinichen's manuscript of *Diana su l'Elba*, pb = partbook(s), Fl. = flute(s), Ob. = oboe(s), Hn. = horn(s), Vn. = violin(s), Va. = viola, B. = bassi, B.c. = basso continuo, *f* = forte, *p* = piano, Ni. = Nisa, Cli. = Climene, Di. = Diana, A = alto, T = tenor, and B = Bass.

No. 1. Sonata

M. 39, Hn. 2, note 9, 16th note in *D*.   M. 46, Vn. 1, note 4, a in pb.   M. 51, Vn. 1, note 13, f' in *D*.   M. 58, Vn. 2, lower voice lacking in pb.   Mm. 59–78, woodwind parts lacking in *D*.   M. 64, Vn. 2, *p* in pb.   M. 78, double-repeat sign at end in *D*.

No. 2. Coro

Mm. 13–31, A, T, and B, missing text was added without notice since the beaming makes clear the distribution of syllables.

No. 3. Aria

Vn., "VV (Senza Hautb:)" noted between the first systems.   M. 12, Vn. 2, *p* in pb.   M. 23, Vn. 1, note 10, *p* in pb; Vn. 2, *p* in pb.   M. 24, Vn. 1, notes 1–8, slurred in *D*. M. 28, Vn. 1, note 9, *f* in *D*.   M. 33, Vn. 1, note 1, *f* in pb. M. 49, Vn. 1, slurs in pb.   M. 51, Vn. 1, notes 5–8, slurs in pb; Va., ♯ lacking in pb.

No. 4. Aria

Aria not numbered in *D*. Vn., "Unis: Flaut. Travers: Flaut. douc: e violini" at beginning of the system in *D*. Vn. 1, "non tanto" penciled in front of "Allegro" in pb.   M. 1, B., "piano sempre" in *D*.   M. 13, Vn. 1, 2, notes 2–4, slurred in *D* (this seems to indicate that Heinichen expected the figure to be slurred in performance, though slurs are lacking in the pb).   M. 76, Di., dotted quarter note in *D*.

No. 5. Aria

It is certain that the oboes rest in mm. 8–16, 20 (beat 2)–29, and 37–47 (and therefore the rest of the aria) because "Violini" (i.e., without oboes) is marked for these sections in the Vn. systems of *D*. The allocation of the Ob. and Vn. parts is unequivocally due to the "Violini" (senza oboi) instructions in the systems of the Vn. in *D*.   M. 8, Vn. 2, *p* in pb.   M. 29, Vn. 1, note 3, fermata penciled in pb.   M. 30, Vn. 2, *f* in pb.   M. 37, Vn. 2, *p* in pb.   M. 47, Vn. 1, note 2, fermata penciled in pb.

Recitative (Nisa)

Mm. 1–9, Ni., B., no ♯ in key signature.   M. 12, Ni., notes 4–7, "Ti vidi si" in libretto.

No. 6. Aria

The designation "Moderato" for the aria is found in Vn. 1 pb. Vn. 1, 2, two-♯ key signature in pb.   M. 2, Vn. 1, *f* in pb.   M. 5, Vn. 2, Va., *p* in pb.   M. 7, Va., *p* in pb. M. 9, Vn. 2, *p* in pb.   M. 10, Va., *f* in pb.   M. 15, Va., *p* in pb.   M. 28, Vn. 1, 2, *p* lacking in pb.   M. 29, Vn. 2, *p* in pb.   M. 30, Vn. 2, notes 1–2, slurred in pb.   M. 32, Vn. 2, notes 1–2, slurred in pb.   M. 43, Vn. 2, *p* in pb.   M. 47, note 8–m. 48, note 1, Vn. 1, 2, slurred in pb.   M. 51, Vn. 2, *f* in pb.   M. 53, Va., *p* in pb.   M. 55, Vn. 1, 2, *p* lacking in pb.   M. 56, Va., *f* in pb.   M. 60, Vn. 2, Va., *p* in pb.   M. 61, Vn. 1, note 1, eighth note in pb.

No. 7. Aria

The instruction "senza Hautb:" is written in the first system of *D*.   M. 9, rhythm is ♪ ♪ ♫♫ in *D* and pb. M. 10, Vn. 1, Va., strokes in pb.   M. 14, Vn. 1, 2, and Va., strokes in pb.   M. 28, Vn. 2, *p* in pb.   M. 51, rhythm is ♪ ♪ ♫♫ in *D* and pb; Vn. 2., *f* in pb.   M. 52, Vn. 1, Va., strokes in pb.   M. 53, Vn. 1, note 1, stroke in pb. M. 54, Vn. 1, 2, and Va., strokes in pb.   M. 56, Vn. 1, Va., strokes in pb.   M. 59, Vn. 2, Va., *p* in pb.   M. 63, Vn. 2, Va., *f* in pb.   M. 67, Vn. 2, Va., *p* in pb.   M. 71, Vn. 2, *p* in pb.   M. 84, Vn. 2, *p* in pb.   M. 81, B.c., note 1, bass figure 6 is below the note.   M. 89, Vn. 2, *p* in pb.   M. 92, Vn. 2, *f* in pb.   M. 97, Vn. 1, *f* in pb.   M. 102, rhythm is ♪ ♫♫♫♫ in *D* and pb.   M. 105, Vn. 1, 2, and Va., note 1, ♯ in pb.   M. 114, Vn. 1, fermata in pb.   M. 115, Vn. 2, *p* in pb.   M. 124, Vn. 1, *p* in pb.

Recitative (Climene/Diana)

M. 14, Cli., note 4 is illegible in *D* (it has been added by the editor in the edition).

No. 8. Aria

Vn. 1, 2, the designation "Moderato" for the aria is lacking in pb.   M. 5, Vn. 2, *p* in pb.   M. 6, Vn. 1, notes 2–3, slur lacking in pb.   M. 8, Vn. 2, *f* in pb.   M. 16, Vn. 2, Va., *p* in pb.   M. 20, Vn. 1, notes 2–3, eighth note d" in pb.   M. 25, instruction "Viol." (that is, "Violini senza Oboi," which means that oboes were employed in the ritornellos).   M. 67, Vn. 2, *p* in pb.   M. 72, Vn. 2, *p* in pb.   M. 74, Vn. 1, notes 2 and 3, eighth note d″ in pb; Vn. 2, *f* in pb.   M. 79, Vn. 2, *p* in pb.   M. 81, Vn. 2, note 3, c′ in pb.   M. 83, Vn. 1, notes 2–4, slurred in pb.   M. 93, note 3–m. 94, note 1, Vn. 1, slur lacking in pb.

Recitative (Diana)

M. 7, Di., notes 3–5, "piacer" in the libretto.

No. 9. Coro

M. 17, Vn. 1, 2, *p* in pb.   M. 25, Vn. 1, 2, *f* in pb.   Mm. 27–40, A, T, and B, missing text was added without notice since the beaming makes clear the distribution of syllables.   M. 41, Vn. 2, *p* in pb.   M. 55, Vn. 1, 2, and Va., *f* in pb.   Mm. 57–68, 89–95, 98–109, A, T, and B, missing text was added without notice since the beaming makes clear the distribution of syllables.

RECENT RESEARCHES IN THE MUSIC OF THE BAROQUE ERA
Christoph Wolff, general editor